UPPER ROOM to GARDEN TOMB

UPPER
ROOM
to
GARDEN
TOMB

Messages for Lent and Easter
on the Passion Narrative in Mark

Herbert E. Hohenstein

AUGSBURG Publishing House • Minneapolis

UPPER ROOM TO GARDEN TOMB
Messages for Lent and Easter on the Passion Narrative in Mark

Copyright © 1984 Augsburg Publishing House

Scripture quotations unless otherwise noted are from the Revised Standard Version of the Bible, copyright 1946, 1952, and 1971 by the Division of Christian Education of the National Council of Churches.

Library of Congress Cataloging in Publication Data

Hohenstein, Herbert E., 1928-
UPPER ROOM TO GARDEN TOMB.

   1. Bible. N.T. Mark XIV-XVI—Sermons.
2. Jesus Christ—Passion—Sermons. 3. Easter—Sermons.
4. Sermons, American. I. Title.
BS2585.4.H64   1984   252'.62   84-21735
ISBN 0-8066-2117-6 (pbk.)

Manufactured in the U.S.A.   APH 10-6840

1 2 3 4 5 6 7 8 9 0 1 2 3 4 5 6 7 8 9

To Ruth
for her constant support,
love, and encouragement.

Contents

Preface

There are three verbs of Lent—*remember, repent,* and *prepare.* During Lent God's people *remember* the events of four days. A Thursday when the Lord Jesus instituted the supper of champions for frightened, burdened, doubt-filled disciples; a Thursday when he literally sweat blood in the Gethsemane garden in his struggle to submit to the Father's mysterious inscrutable will; then came the stripes and spit and scorn of his trial. A Friday when he hung a broken bloody corpse on a cross, abandoned by his friends and deserted by his God. A Saturday when his breathless body lay still and sealed in that stone cold tomb. And finally a Sunday when he walked right through his boulder-blocked grave door out into the woods and

fields and forests of endless and immortal life
to be our coffin-conqueror and death-destroyer.
That is what God's people remember during
Lent.

And then they *repent*. Remembering inevitably leads to repentance. In the familiar Lenten
hymn the author prays: "Grant that I thy passion view with repentant grieving." And so to
turn to the cross during Lent is also to turn
from our sins to God in genuine sorrow and
repentance.

The final verb of Lent is *prepare*. Get ready
for the joy of Easter.

There is something significant about the
number 40. Ancient Israel spent 40 long agonizing years being readied by God for the joys
of the Promised Land. Jesus spent 40 days in
the cruel and savage wilderness preparing himself for the joy of victory over the defeated Satan. Even so we spend 40 days in the desert of
our Lenten disciplines getting ready for the joy
of Easter. It is good to do so.

The sermons that follow are an attempt to aid
both pastor and people in their disciplined ef-
forts to practice and live the verbs of Lent. The
focus is on the passion history of our Lord according to St. Mark, with individual sermons
concentrating chronologically on segments of

that story. My hope is that by way of the preached Word the hearers will engage in a meaningful companionship with the Savior as he goes his divinely ordained way from the upper room to the garden tomb.

1

ASH WEDNESDAY

At Supper
with Jesus

¹²And on the first day of Unleavened Bread, when they sacrificed the passover lamb, his disciples said to him, "Where will you have us go and prepare for you to eat the passover?" ¹³And he sent two of his disciples, and said to them, "Go into the city, and a man carrying a jar of water will meet you; follow him, ¹⁴and wherever he enters, say to the householder, 'The Teacher says, Where is my guest room, where I am to eat the passover with my disciples?' ¹⁵And he will show you a large upper room furnished and ready; there prepare for us." ¹⁶And the disciples set out and went to the city, and found it as he had told them; and they prepared the passover.

[17]And when it was evening he came with the twelve. [18]And as they were at the table eating, Jesus said, "Truly, I say to you, one of you will betray me, one who is eating with me." [19]They began to be sorrowful, and to say to him one after another, "Is it I?" [20]He said to them, "It is one of the twelve, one who is dipping bread into the dish with me. [21]For the Son of man goes as it is written of him, but woe to that man by whom the Son of man is betrayed! It would have been better for that man if he had not been born."

[22]And as they were eating, he took bread, and blessed, and broke it, and gave it to them, and said, "Take; this is my body." [23]And he took a cup, and when he had given thanks he gave it to them, and they all drank of it. [24]And he said to them, "This is my blood of the covenant, which is poured out for many. [25]Truly, I say to you, I shall not drink again of the fruit of the vine until that day when I drink it new in the kingdom of God."

Mark 14:12-25

Our Lenten journey to the cross with Jesus begins. St. Mark is our guide, the words of Christ's passion story our path. We commence our journey *at supper with Jesus. (Mark 14:12-16 is read.)*

You can't help but notice how firmly in command and control the Master is. He gives the orders, issues the instructions, orchestrates the events. They don't take him into their hands; he takes them into his.

And so it still is. Passions and Gethsemanes and Golgothas don't just happen to you, without his will, apart from the Master's wise, loving, beautiful, and magnificent plan. In all of your agonizing and bitter Good Fridays the King of Calvary is still in command and control, making it all turn out for your temporal and eternal victory and blessing. How can it be otherwise? Behold him bloody dead and lifeless on that cruel and bitter tree. If his love for you is that deep, fierce, fervent, passionate, and self-giving, then surely a love like that must be at the heart of everything that happens in your life, even the dark and unbearable mysteries.

There is also a warning in these words: look out for leaven. During the Feast of Unleavened Bread all leaven or yeast had to be removed from Jewish homes, because leaven signified sin and evil. You have the Bread of Life, don't you? Or more accurately, Jesus, the Bread of Life, has you in his nail-scarred hands. And he will continue through gospel Word and communion bread and wine to give you the power to resist the yeast of sin that threatens ever so quietly and imperceptibly to rise and grow and spread in your hearts and lives. You've got that Living Bread to help you get rid of the yeast, to celebrate an uninterrupted lifelong Feast of Unleavened Bread.

Now on to the next event in the story. (*Read verses 17-21.*)

They are evening meals, both the Jewish Passover and the Christian Lord's Supper. Is there anything theologically significant about that? Does the very word *supper* remind us that the day of life may well be almost over, that the time for us to do the Father's will and be about his business is short and fleeting, that the swiftly flying hours dare not be wasted or frittered away in peripheral piffle, procrastination, unfaithfulness, or majoring in minors? It is evening, and the day is far spent. Duties wait to be done; burdens wait to be borne; people wait to be loved. Come, eat and drink at Christ's table and be converted from perpetual procrastinators into veritable dynamos.

It should also be noted that the Master eats with betrayers and deserters, both before and after their betrayals and desertions. Before the little group heads for the temptations and trials of the Gethsemane Garden, the Savior eats with them, shares his body and blood with them, gives his very self to them, thereby hoping to make them brave and strong and triumphant in the dark and difficult hour. It fails; it doesn't work. They all betray, deny, forsake, and desert him, even—and especially—the proud-talking Peter.

After the resurrection, the grave-conquering Lord again eats with his disciples, holds some post-Easter picnics by the Galilean lake. What does it mean? It means forgiveness, restoration, renewed fellowship. When a Jew eats with someone, it is his or her way of saying: "I love you; we are eternal companions and friends."

Now you know what the Lord's Supper really is all about. It is the meal in which the Master wants to make you valiant and victorious in every Gethsemane or Good Friday of your life. And that's the way it often works. The Holy Eucharist is indeed your supper of champions, a meal that makes you more than conquerors in the trials, conflicts, and battles. But when, like the disciples in Gethsemane, you falter and fail and fall, your risen Lord continues to hold post-Easter picnics with you in the blessed sacrament assuring you that you are still loved, treasured, and forgiven. And from those Eucharistic picnics you rise to return to the same old battles and burdens with renewed courage and commitment.

Now to the closing words of the story. (*Read verses 22-25.*) It is a fact that we become what we eat. Is that why we so frequently partake of the Lord's Supper, because we so desperately want to become what we eat? We want to be the incarnate, flesh-and-blood Christ to those about us, being what he was, going where he went, doing what he did, saying what he said, turning the other cheek, washing people's feet in humble love, fighting fire with water, dying for enemies, being living loaves of bread who are consumed and devoured that others might live. Is that why we come to the communion table, so that we might become what we eat— the body of Christ?

There's good news at the end of the meal. The Lord Jesus tells us that every sacramental celebration is a reminder of the happy feast to come, the feast that begins when he returns to devour death and sorrow on that glad and triumphant resurrection morning. What a Eucharist that will be, as we dine not on bread and wine, but on pain and death, those two monsters that now make such hearty and constant meals out of us. What a Communion, what a supper with Jesus that will be!

2

With the Savior in the Garden

²⁶And when they had sung a hymn, they went out to the Mount of Olives. ²⁷And Jesus said to them, "You will all fall away; for it is written, 'I will strike the shepherd, and the sheep will be scattered.' ²⁸But after I am raised up, I will go before you to Galilee." ²⁹Peter said to him, "Even though they all fall away, I will not." ³⁰And Jesus said to him, "Truly, I say to you, this very night, before the cock crows twice, you will deny me three times." ³¹But he said vehemently, "If I must die with you, I will not deny you." And they all said the same.

³²And they went to a place which was called Gethsemane; and he said to his disciples, "Sit here, while I pray." ³³And he took with him Peter and

James and John, and began to be greatly distressed and troubled. ³⁴And he said to them, "My soul is very sorrowful, even to death; remain here, and watch." ³⁵And going a little farther, he fell on the ground and prayed that, if it were possible, the hour might pass from him. ³⁶And he said, "Abba, Father, all things are possible to thee; remove this cup from me; yet not what I will, but what thou wilt." ³⁷And he came and found them sleeping, and he said to Peter, "Simon, are you asleep? Could you not watch one hour? ³⁸Watch and pray that you may not enter into temptation; the spirit indeed is willing, but the flesh is weak." ³⁹And again he went away and prayed, saying the same words. ⁴⁰And again he came and found them sleeping, for their eyes were very heavy; and they did not know what to answer him. ⁴¹And he came the third time, and said to them, "Are you still sleeping and taking your rest? It is enough; the hour has come; the Son of man is betrayed into the hands of sinners. ⁴²Rise, let us be going; see, my betrayer is at hand."

Mark 14:26-42

During these Lenten days we are pondering the passion of our Lord according to St. Mark. Now we are *with the Savior in the Garden.* (*Read verses 26-31.*) As the powers of darkness and hell drew ominously near, as the little group walked, perhaps with hesitant and reluctant steps, into the teeth of trouble and the jaws of danger, trial, and anguish, they resolutely sang a song. Of course! For hymns were a joyous part of the Passover celebration.

But perhaps on this night as they headed for the darkness, dangers, and sorrows of Gethsemane, the singing of that song was more than just the faithful observance of a religious tradition. It was power from on high to be strong and brave in the midst of the advancing armies of Satan and hell.

Thus it has always been for God's people down through the centuries. Think of Paul and Silas in the darkness of that Philippian jail, their backs beaten and bleeding from the Roman scourge as a result of their courageous testimony to the Christ, their fate and future uncertain, with martyrdom a near and likely possibility. And what happened? At midnight, we are told, when the darkness was the deepest, they suddenly broke forth into glad hymns of praise. Now how could they do that? They could do that because they were Easter people. They were sure that they had a grave-conquering Master, a death-defeating Lord. And so they sang in the midst of their miseries. God's teakettles, that's what they were. The hotter the water, the more loudly they sang.

Shall we not do the same? Or is it possible that some of us are still living on the wrong side of Easter—the dark, gloomy, sad, depressing Good Friday side? Can it really be that some of us are still sorrowing and sighing, moaning and groaning, grieving, fearing, worrying, and despairing as if Easter had never happened, as if that great glad day were only a myth, as if our resurrected Savior still lies buried and entombed in some unmarked Judean grave? Well, he lives, and as you head for Gethsemane, you can sing.

Now notice the prediction the Master makes as they walk to the Mount of Olives: "You will all fall away." How do you think he said that—with obvious and unmistakable bitterness, anger, surprise, and disappointment in his voice? Or did he say it in a voice filled with compassion, love, forgiveness, and understanding? Where did you ever get the idea that Jesus Christ doesn't know, cannot comprehend, how tough and hard and difficult and impossible it is to be eternally true and triumphant in every trial, to be unswervingly faithful in every bout and battle with the Evil One? His own swiftly approaching anguish in the Gethsemane Garden makes it comfortingly clear that he knows how easy it is to fail and fall away when Satan's fiery darts begin to fly. And that is why forgiveness is always there, enabling and empowering us to pick up the pieces of our broken lives, our shattered hopes and dreams, and despite the defeats, disappointments, and failures, once again to begin anew.

Did you hear that ridiculous vow uttered by that arrogant disciple? "If I must die with you, I will not deny you." And that is precisely why he did deny his Lord three times. Proudly he boasted that it could never happen, that he could never sink or stoop that low, be guilty of such a despicable, heinous offense. By now we should have learned never to think or say: "I will *never* do that," or "That will *never* happen to me." For such thoughts and words reveal that falls and betrayals are near.

The story continues. (*Read verses 32-42.*) Suffering is a lonely, solitary burden and experience. The sharp, intense agonies and sorrows he bore in the Gethsemane Garden were his alone to endure—as they always are. People can surround us, be there with us, and try as best they can to sympathize, empathize, and identify with us, but they cannot carry the cross or load for us.

Is that why death sometimes frightens and terrifies us? We know that although when we breathe our last, we may be surrounded by loved ones and friends, we must still die alone. No one can do the dying with or for us. Yet, does the divine Shepherd lie when he promises to be with us as we take that first reluctant and hesitant step into the dark and gloomy valley? Of course not. It's always a pair, a twosome—dying you and your companion-God who will lead you safely through that dark valley into the green pastures of endless joy and life.

Suffering may be a lonely and solitary experience, but it can be shared with others. That's why the Master took Peter, James, and John with him to the Gethsemane anguish. He did not want to be alone—nor do we or the people around us. When it's time for Gethsemane or Golgotha, no one should have to be there alone, neglected, forgotten, unaided, uncomforted. You won't be like the disciples, will you, sleeping while those nearby suffer intense sorrows abandoned and alone?

And sometimes all you can do is to be there. Jesus wasn't asking for words from his companions, just the comfort, strength, and reassurance of their presence in his hour of anguish. Just your physical presence—the love and understanding in your tear-filled eyes, the holding of that heartbroken person in your arms—that and nothing more is needed, wanted, deeply desired, and appreciated.

This episode in the garden also provides the secret to a happy, content, and triumphant life. That blessing becomes ours only as we confess with the Lord Jesus: "Not my will, but thine be done." How can there be lasting peace in our hearts and lives when we constantly fight and battle against God and his good, though mysterious, plans and paths for us? Of course, no one desires, relishes, or anticipates the darkness and horror of Gethsemane or Calvary. But if it is our loving, guiding God who brings us to those places of torment and agony, then, following in the footsteps of our Savior, we will submit and surrender ourselves to a heavenly Father who still knows how to bring good out of evil, joy out of sorrow, blessings out of burdens, crowns out of crosses, life out of death, and who will at last turn every bitter Good Friday into a glad, bright, and victorious Easter morning.

3

The Arrested
Savior

[43]And immediately, while he was still speaking, Judas came, one of the twelve, and with him a crowd with swords and clubs, from the chief priests and the scribes and the elders. [44]Now the betrayer had given them a sign, saying, "The one I shall kiss is the man; seize him and lead him away under guard." [45]And when he came, he went up to him at once, and said, "Master!" And he kissed him. [46]And they laid hands on him and seized him. [47]But one of those who stood by drew his sword, and struck the slave of the high priest and cut off his ear. [48]And Jesus said to them, "Have you come out as against a robber, with swords and clubs to capture me? [49]Day after day I was with you in the temple

teaching, and you did not seize me. But let the scriptures be fulfilled." ⁵⁰And they all forsook him, and fled.

⁵¹And a young man followed him, with nothing but a linen cloth about his body; and they seized him, ⁵²but he left the linen cloth and ran away naked.

Mark 14:43-52

Our Lenten journey continues as we behold *the arrested Savior. (Read Mark 14:43-52.)* There was a kiss of death. It was, of course, the kiss Judas planted on the cheek of Jesus.

Why did he do it? Was it greed that moved him? Is it possible that people will abandon and betray friends for the sake of money? Or maybe Judas planted the kiss of death on the cheek of Jesus because *he* felt betrayed, convinced that his Master was a false Messiah and had best be executed rather than continue his disastrous deception of the people. Or maybe it was fear that controlled the betrayer, fear that Jesus was showing unmistakable signs of becoming an anti-Roman revolutionary who would most certainly incur the wrath of the authorities and eventually bring a bloodbath to the land. By delivering his Master to the cross, Judas would save him from himself and the nation from certain destruction.

Or maybe Judas had no choice in the matter. Maybe he was just plain doomed and destined to do what he did. Was that perhaps the implied meaning of those mysterious words uttered by the Master a few hours earlier at the supper table: "Woe to that man by whom the Son of man is betrayed! It would have been better for that man if he had not been born" (v. 21). How can one escape, impede, or negate the will and plan of almighty God? Far from blaming Judas, maybe we should just plain pity him.

The kiss of death! Sadly we say that it was only the first of a long and seemingly endless succession of betrayers' kisses. "Master," we confess with our lips every Sunday in our worship rites and rituals, and then proceed to betray him the rest of the week with our lives—our thoughts and words and deeds that are something less than righteous, godly, and Christlike.

But of course that is why he was betrayed in the garden, nailed to the cross, raised from the tomb. It happened so that betrayers like us might have God's forgiveness. And then in the power of that pardon we begin anew our lifelong struggle to be faithful and committed to him who died for us and rose again.

The kiss of death was followed by a drawn sword. Peter was the one who drew that sword in an impetuous yet well-intentioned gesture to defend and deliver his friend and Master. But, as another evangelist informs us, Jesus would have none of it. He quickly commanded his sword-swinging disciple to sheathe his weapon.

Are we ever justified in being violent for the sake of a righteous cause? Can love ever compel us to kill, whether in defense of ourselves or another, or on orders from the state? Said the cheek-turning Christ to his sword-swinging follower: "Put your sword in its place."

Now, Lord, be reasonable. You know very well we cannot survive, let alone flourish and prosper, if we take your words seriously, and faithfully attempt to live and practice them. It's kill or be killed in this fiercely competitive, dog-eat-dog, survival-of-the-fittest-and-strongest world. What do you expect us to be—lambs in the midst of wolves and lions? "Precisely," he responds. "For that is what I was for you—the sacrificial, life-losing Lamb. I am your model and power to do and be the same."

And so maybe it isn't a matter of survival. If we begin to practice cheek-turning, non-sword-swinging love, we say we cannot survive. If we attempt to conquer hate with love, subdue violence with nonviolence, fight fire with water, we will probably die. But maybe that is not the issue. Rather maybe this is what it is all about—being uncompromisingly faithful to the cheek-turning, nonviolent Christ who told us that we will find our lives only if we lose them and that sword swinging is out for those who are in his discipleship circle.

"Put your sword in its place." Good advice for violent, agressive, hot-tempered people who are so quick to retaliate and get even, to fight, battle, and bully their way through life, to climb and scramble to the top at all costs, even if it means the sacrifice of principles and integrity and great hurt to other people.

First the kiss of death, then the drawing of a sword, and now a glorious irony: he who came from God to rob us of nothing, but only to give everything, including his very life for our sake and salvation, is now seized and taken as a robber. The one person—yes, the only person—who could never be mistaken for a robber, because he is so totally self-giving, is now violently apprehended and begins those first agonizing steps toward the cross on which he will be robbed of everything—his clothes, his dignity, his friends, his life, even his God. And by that robbery of the cross you and I live forever.

A kiss of death, a drawn sword, a glorious irony, and then another magnificent surrender to the mysterious will of the Father! "Let the scriptures be fulfilled," shouted the captured Christ and willingly and submissively began to walk with his captors to the house of Caiaphas and the Calvary hill.

May God give us that Christlike faith as we head for whatever Calvarys and crosses may be waiting for us. The Father is in charge, command, and control, and there is always an Easter at the end of every dark and dismal road—even the one called death. And so we surrender and submit—but always with hope in our hearts.

A kiss of death, a drawn sword, a glorious irony, a sterling faith, but then by contrast, some sad and wretched unfaithfulness: "And they all forsook him, and fled." These are the men who only a few hours earlier had so vigorously and vehemently asserted their undying faithfulness, had vowed and promised they would die before ever they would desert him. Of course, such pride is always the first step on the road to denial, unfaithfulness, and desertion.

Well, *they* may have forsaken and abandoned *him*—but he never abandoned them! Out of the tomb he came on Easter morning. "I'll meet you in Galilee," he said through the lips of the resurrection angel. And meet them he did, thereby declaring the fellowship unbroken, despite their unpardonable desertion.

More than that! The risen Master even ate with those unfaithful followers. It was his way of saying: "I still love you, forgive you, and am your friend forever."

And he still eats with unfaithful disciples, offers himself to denying, deserting disciples in every communion meal. And the message is still the same: "Oh, faithless, forsaking disciples, I love you, forgive you, and am your eternal friend."

Now, in the power of that meal, that forgiving word, go forth to be his undyingly faithful followers.

4

The Judge on Trial

⁵³And they led Jesus to the high priest; and all the chief priests and the elders and the scribes were assembled. ⁵⁴And Peter had followed him at a distance, right into the courtyard of the high priest; and he was sitting with the guards, and warming himself at the fire. ⁵⁵Now the chief priests and the whole council sought testimony against Jesus to put him to death; but they found none. ⁵⁶For many bore false witness against him, and their witness did not agree. ⁵⁷And some stood up and bore false witness against him, saying, ⁵⁸"We heard him say, 'I will destroy this temple that is made with hands, and in three days I will build another, not made with hands.' " ⁵⁹Yet not even so did their testimony agree. ⁶⁰And the high priest stood up in the midst, and asked Jesus, "Have you no answer to make? What is it that these men testify against you?" ⁶¹But he was silent and made no answer. Again the high

priest asked him, "Are you the Christ, the Son of the Blessed?" ⁶²And Jesus said, "I am; and you will see the Son of man seated at the right hand of Power, and coming with the clouds of heaven." ⁶³And the high priest tore his garments, and said, "Why do we still need witnesses? ⁶⁴You have heard his blasphemy. What is your decision? "And they all condemned him as deserving death. ⁶⁵And some began to spit on him, and to cover his face, and to strike him, saying to him, "Prophesy!" And the guards received him with blows.

⁶⁶And as Peter was below in the courtyard, one of the maids of the high priest came; ⁶⁷and seeing Peter warming himself, she looked at him, and said, "You also were with the Nazarene, Jesus." ⁶⁸But he denied it, saying, "I neither know nor understand what you mean." And he went out into the gateway. ⁶⁹And the maid saw him, and began again to say to the bystanders, "This man is one of them." ⁷⁰But again he denied it. And after a little while again the bystanders said to Peter, "Certainly you are one of them; for you are a Galilean." ⁷¹But he began to invoke a curse on himself and to swear, "I do not know this man of whom you speak." ⁷²And immediately the cock crowed a second time. And Peter remembered how Jesus had said to him, "Before the cock crows twice, you will deny me three times." And he broke down and wept.

Mark 14:53-72

What is this that we behold tonight? The one who normally presides at the trial and then passes sentence is himself in the dock. It is *the judge on trial*. (*Read Mark 14:53-72*).

We turn our attention first to those who tried him, the religious authorities. Why did they hate him so? Was it because they were jealous of his obvious popularity with the people? Or maybe they felt threatened by him. Perhaps they saw him as an insurrectionist, an ecclesiastical and political rebel, whose radical philosophy and practices might well invite the wrath of Rome and bring a bloodbath to the nation. Maybe the high priest was right: it would be better that one man should die rather than to allow the entire nation to perish. Or were these religious authorities infuriated by this backwoods upstart who was going around breaking their hallowed laws and time-honored traditions? Whatever their motives and reasons, at last they had the hated one in their hands and were determined to do away with him.

But really the judge wasn't on trial; the jury was. He wasn't standing before them; they were standing before him. Thus it always is when an authority that is genuine and legitimate and divinely ordained confronts self-appointed judges. Bach is never on trial before the concert audience; it is the audience that awaits his sentence. Michelangelo is never on trial before the art class; it is they who must accept his verdict. So here Jesus, with his self-authenticating religious and moral pronouncements and insights, together with the towering stature of his personality, is not on trial before these little men; they are on trial before him. And when all is said and done, the last chapter composed, the final sentence written, only his verdict stands eternally.

How prejudiced the jury was! In fact, their minds were made up even before they had captured him. In their hearts they had already pronounced the death sentence—even before they had summoned the first witness into the courtroom.

Yet who are we to point accusing condemning fingers at that Jewish jury? Does the anti-Semitism that frequently poisons our hearts and that reached its tragic and terrible climax in Hitler's Holocaust begin right here, at the trial of Jesus? Have not Gentile Christians down through the centuries lovelessly and hatefully accused Jews of being "Christ killers" and treated them with shameful scorn and contempt? "Not I," you say. Yet what are the words that escape from your lips after that lucrative deal? "Boy, did I ever *Jew* him down!" Whoever heard of saying: "Boy, did I *Gentile* him down"? In our Gentile pride and prejudice we speculate on whether Jews will go to heaven, forgetting that they are God's chosen people and that the very Savior we trust and adore is a crucified and risen *Jew*.

From the jury in the high priest's house we now turn to the disciple in the courtyard. The first thing we note about him is that he followed the Lord Jesus at a distance. That's the safe and smart way, of course—stay close enough to the Master to convince yourself that you are still his faithful follower, but not so close that you expose yourself to all those risks and perils and sacrifices of passionate, all-out discipleship. Lukewarm will do just fine. Let no one ever accuse me of being a fanatic.

The name of that distance-following disciple was Rock—or Peter, if you will. But Rock was now a reed, a windblown blade of grass. There was no strength or courage or commitment in him at all. Why? What happened to him? Pride did him in. He had just boasted and bragged that he would never deny his master, and that's what made him do it. Panic overcame him. And we do all sorts of stupid irrational and cowardly things when we push panic buttons. His hostile environment caused him to fall. We know how true that is, and yet we sometimes consciously and deliberately stroll into the jaws of temptation. Then there was crowd pressure. They said he was an outsider, a Galilean, not one of them. Nobody wants to be treated as an outsider. I'll do anything, even sacrifice my principles and integrity, rather than to be excluded from the group. Or was it self-concern that made him deny the Master? "I've got to survive at all costs." If it's ever a case of denial or death—denial of my convictions, my Christ—or execution, denial would be a most tempting, almost irresistible choice. Not everyone can be a man or woman for all seasons, especially when the executioner waits in the wings.

And so Rock was a reed that night and denied his Master. But the story doesn't end there. The last words of the text are these: "He broke down and wept." The crowing cock brought him to his senses, jolted and jarred him out of his spiritual stupor. For that crowing rooster reminded him of the words of Jesus spoken just a few hours before, warning words about a triple denial that would be uttered by the time that crowing bird had heralded the dawn of the new day.

That's always the first step out of the quicksand and quagmire of denial and betrayal: remembering the warning, loving, forgiving words of Jesus. And then come the tears, the bitter tears of repentance, that lead to restoration and renewal. Were there tears in the eyes of the repentant Judas? No matter. For tears or not, he went out and hanged himself, not knowing or believing that the very man he betrayed was destined to hang on a tree for his pardon and salvation. There were tears in the eyes of Peter, but he did not go out and hang himself. Someone intervened, and to that someone we now turn.

Jesus, the judge, endured it all—the spit, the blows, the injustice, the scorn—in admirable and majestic silence, like the Lamb that he was. They sheared God's lamb, not just of his wool, but of his clothes, his dignity, his life, even his God, as he suffered the terrors and torments of his trial and cross to make us God's own forever.

Are we, like him, dumb before our shearers, or do we let all the world know how badly we've been hurt and mistreated? To be sure, there is a time to speak and a time to be silent. Our fervent prayer is that God's Spirit will ever guide, control, and enlighten us so that we know when to do which.

Really, he didn't have to speak, to give answer to that questioning high priest. He let his deeds do all the talking. They knew what he had done: how he had driven demons out of possessed and tormented bodies, restored hearing to the deaf and sight to the blind, cured epileptics and the mentally ill, and made the paralyzed and crippled walk and leap and run again—yes, how he had even revived and raised the dead. They knew how he had let his deeds do the talking.

Do people still know that about us? Sermons are to be seen as well as heard, and the most eloquent speech is still the loving life of the speaker. Or put another way, let there always be a beautiful wedding between what we say and what we do. Divorce here is unthinkable, impossible, and wholly unacceptable.

But he did speak when the proper time came: "Again the high priest asked him, 'Are you the Christ, the Son of the Blessed?' And Jesus said, 'I am; and you will see the Son of man seated at the right hand of Power, and coming with the clouds of heaven.' " That's when he should have shut up and remained silent—if he knew what was good and safe for him. Opening his mouth then meant sure and certain death. But he spoke and confessed and got killed.

Sometimes it's very costly to speak, to speak up for your convictions, your Christ, to say the honest and true word. It can cost you popularity, money, fun, your job. It can bring you criticism, hatred, hostility, contempt, disgrace, even death. Just ask Jesus, or John the Baptist, or Joan of Arc, or Thomas More, or Dietrich Bonhoeffer what it costs to speak up. These people all sealed their courageous words with their blood.

But what if you're not like that? What if you're more like triple-denying Peter? What then? Why, then you can expect what he received from the Savior: the forgiving look, the loving understanding glance. No it's not there in Mark, but it is in Luke (Luke 22:61). Praise God for that. For it is that compassionate pardoning look that inspires us to put all our denials, desertions, and betrayals behind us and begin again to walk life's path with the Master.

5

Condemned
by the State

[1]And as soon as it was morning the chief priests, with the elders and scribes, and the whole council held a consultation; and they bound Jesus and led him away and delivered him to Pilate. [2]And Pilate asked him, "Are you the King of the Jews?" And he answered him, "You have said so." [3]And the chief priests accused him of many things. [4]And Pilate again asked him, "Have you no answer to make? See how many charges they bring against you." [5]But Jesus made no further answer, so that Pilate wondered.

[6]Now at the feast he used to release for them one prisoner for whom they asked. [7]And among the rebels in prison, who had committed murder in the insurrection, there was a man called Barabbas. [8]And the crowd came up and began to ask Pilate to do

as he was wont to do for them. ⁹And he answered them, "Do you want me to release for you the King of the Jews?" ¹⁰For he perceived that it was out of envy that the chief priests had delivered him up. ¹¹But the chief priests stirred up the crowd to have him release for them Barabbas instead. ¹²And Pilate again said to them, "Then what shall I do with the man whom you call the King of the Jews?" ¹³And they cried out again, "Crucify him." ¹⁴And Pilate said to them, "Why, what evil has he done?" But they shouted all the more, "Crucify him." ¹⁵So Pilate, wishing to satisfy the crowd, released for them Barabbas; and having scourged Jesus, he delivered him to be crucified.

¹⁶And the soldiers led him away inside the palace (that is, the praetorium); and they called together the whole battalion. ¹⁷And they clothed him in a purple cloak, and plaiting a crown of thorns they put it on him. ¹⁸And they began to salute him, "Hail, King of the Jews!" ¹⁹And they struck his head with a reed, and spat upon him, and they knelt down in homage to him. ²⁰And when they had mocked him, they stripped him of the purple cloak, and put his own clothes on him. And they led him out to crucify him.

Mark 15:1-20

Our Lenten journey continues, and we behold the Savior *condemned by the state*.

The second trial begins. (*Read Mark 15:1-5.*) Of course, that's the way it had to be. They had no legal power to execute him, so they delivered their prisoner into the hands of the Roman governor.

Is it possible that at least a few members of the Jewish council were glad that's the way it was? Now his blood wouldn't be on their hands. Pilate would do their dirty work for them. He would be their scapegoat and take the fault, guilt, and blame for their murder of this innocent man.

The scenario is all too familiar. It began in a garden when Adam tried to pin the rap for his transgression on his wife, and Eve pointed the accusing finger at the snake and, thereby, indirectly at God.

When I blow it, goof up, commit those monumental mistakes and blunders, when I fall and fail, it's never my fault. Blame my wife or husband or parents or heredity or environment or bad luck or the stars or God. But it's never my fault. Oh, yes, I thought I made a mistake once, but I was wrong.

This business of attempting to hide behind the trees of our excuses and rationalizations has been going on since Adam and Eve first did it in Paradise Garden centuries ago. When will we ever learn that there is only one tree behind which we can legitimately hide when we offend people and our God? It is the tree which God himself planted on the top of Calvary's hill, the tree on which his own dear Son hung and bled and died to take our guilt away.

The trial continues. (*Read Mark 15:6-15.*) The crowd was confronted with a choice—Jesus or Barabbas. They made the wrong choice. Do we? All life long it seems to be Jesus or someone or something else: Jesus or money, Jesus or fun, Jesus or popularity, Jesus or job.

Once a man came to the Master and volunteered to be his disciple if the Savior would only permit him first to go and bury his dead father— certainly a most reasonable and understandable request! And Jesus said: "Let the dead bury the dead. You follow me." How harsh and cruel and coldhearted and unloving can you get! What was our Lord saying? "Nothing or no one dare ever mean more to you than me, being my follower, being faithful and loyal and devoted to me." As long as some thing or some one means more to us than our Savior, we do not yet have life's priorities straight and properly arranged. It is only when we begin to realize that with the gift of that crucified and risen Man God has filled the little cup of our life to the very top and brim, and that everything else we receive and enjoy—from loved ones to a good golf game—is really only a blessed bonus and overflow, only then do we begin to view life and tears and laughter in their proper perspective. For then we see what counts and matters and lasts eternally.

Now reflect with me for a few moments on Pilate. We might say that here was a man whose good intentions somehow never seemed to get off the ground. "He's innocent, and I should really release him," Pilate said. He knew what was demanded of him, what he ought to have done, but didn't do it.

Are there any "I should" people in the audience? "I should do this," and "I should do that," they say, but somehow the good and noble intentions never get translated into action. They always get short-circuited before they reach tongue or hands or feet to become words and deeds of compassion and love. One of these days the opportunity and the people won't be there, and it will be too late to love, too late to turn those eternally present good intentions into kind actions for others. When Jesus hung dead on the cross, it was too late for Pilate to release him.

Was Pilate a crowd pleaser? Did he permit and allow the crowd to influence, govern, and dictate his actions? I wonder if there are any crowd pleasers among us. That need not be bad. Sometimes it is good to listen to those around us, to heed their counsel and advice, to accept and act on their suggestions for change and improvement. Sometimes the crowd can be the voice of God to us.

But not always. Some people suffer from a seemingly fatal and incurable case of "herditis." They have made the herd, the group, the crowd their god, and whatever this "god" says, they do in blind and mindless obedience. That kind of "herditis" can erode and destroy faith in, and faithfulness to, the Master.

Was Pilate a coward? Is that why he condemned Christ to be crucified—he had no spine, no backbone, no courage? Are there no cowards among us? Is there no one present who has ever compromised his or her conscience, integrity, or principles for the sake of a momentary pleasure or out of fear of unpopularity or persecution or loss of money or job? No Pilates in the audience? Everybody always has the courage of his or her convictions?

Now a word on the crowd. It seems that in their case the larynx had replaced the mind. All they could do was to shout and yell and scream that he was guilty, whether there was evidence or not.

The story is told of a custodian who on a certain Saturday afternoon while cleaning the pastor's study happened to lay eyes on the next day's sermon lying on the pastor's desk. His eyes bugged out as he read these words in the margin next to one of the paragraphs: "Argument weak here. Yell like mad."

Sometimes that's how it is with us. Loud and raised voices only betray the absence of substance, sound argument, and reason. And sometimes when the larynx replaces the mind, great evil is done.

Finally, a few words on the Roman soldiers. (*Read Mark 15:16-20.*) What of the soldiers who mocked him? Theirs was a burlesque, a charade of allegiance to the King. They honored him with their lips and then despised him with their deeds. Are there any Christians like that, people who confess the King with their lips and then deny him with their lives? But, of course, that is why the King was standing before these mocking soldiers in the first place. That is why the crowd and Pilate condemned him to the cross. That is why he hung on that torture tree and rose from that garden grotto. He did it for us who, with the people in this story—the crowd, Pilate, the soldiers—commit all the crimes we've been sadly rehearsing.

The only person we haven't been talking about, the one who stands silently in the background while everybody else does all the shouting and acting, that one person is the most important of all. For his death and resurrection bring God's pardon and new life to past and contemporary crowds and Pilates and soldiers who commit their unspeakable crimes against that innocent and pathetic Good Friday victim. Now, in the power of that pardon bid your guilt good-bye and arise from the ashes of your failures and sins to be God's new people.

6

At Skull Hill

²¹And they compelled a passer-by, Simon of Cyrene, who was coming in from the country, the father of Alexander and Rufus, to carry his cross. ²²And they brought him to the place called Golgotha (which means the place of a skull). ²³And they offered him wine mingled with myrrh; but he did not take it. ²⁴And they crucified him, and divided his garments among them, casting lots for them, to decide what each should take. ²⁵And it was the third hour, when they crucified him. ²⁶And the inscription of the charge against him read, "The King of the Jews." ²⁷And with him they crucified two robbers, one on his right and one on his left. ²⁹And those who passed by derided him, wagging their heads,

and saying, "Aha! You who would destroy the temple and build it in three days, [30]save yourself, and come down from the cross!" [31]So also the chief priests mocked him to one another with the scribes, saying, "He saved others; he cannot save himself. [32]Let the Christ, the King of Israel, come down now from the cross, that we may see and believe." Those who were crucified with him also reviled him.

Mark 15:21-32

Our Lenten journey begins to come to an end. At last we arrive *at Skull Hill*. (*Read Mark 15:21-32*.)

There was great exposure at Skull Hill. The cross completely exposed the Christ. The condemned person was stripped of his clothes and nailed naked to the torment tree. It is unthinkable that he who clothes the lilies of the field with such radiant and unsurpassed beauty should hang unclothed on a cross. It is unbearable that he who covers you with the robe of his own righteousness should hang naked on the Calvary tree.

The cross exposes the Christ, exposes him as a criminal. For only criminals were crucified by Rome. Can we even begin to grasp and comprehend the offense of it all? For us the cross has understandably become the symbol of hope and glory, victory, forgiveness, and salvation. It was not such for those first-century people who first heard the foolishness proclaimed by the apostles.

It would be like someone bursting on the scene today trying to persuade us that the criminal the authorities had just executed in the gas chamber was none other than God himself, that the shameful execution was actually the hour of God's glory and triumph, and that the death of this criminal was the world's only hope of salvation. What sense does that make? What we should do is get rid of all crosses and start hanging electric chairs or miniature gas chambers or gallows or guillotines or firing squads around our neck or on our walls at home, and maybe then the nonsense and foolishness of it all would begin to sink in. But it is God's foolishness, and that makes it wiser than all the wisdom of this world and well worth believing.

The cross exposes Christ as a criminal. And should not such exposure make us more compassionate toward all criminals? How can we continue to treat criminals as animals and sub-humans, feeling only hatred, suspicion, and mistrust toward them, subjecting them to all sorts of despicable and inhumane treatment during their imprisonment, while at the same time we place all our hope for salvation in a crucified criminal? What can you do to hasten the much-needed reformation of our nation's criminal-justice system?

The cross is also the greatest exposure of God. In fact, when one moves six inches from the cross, God becomes an insoluble mystery. There is only one place to go when you can't make any sense out of your life and your world, when everything is so utterly unfathomable and mysterious and you keep hurling that anguished "Why, Lord, why?" to an apparently blind, deaf, and dumb God. There is only one place to go then, and that is Calvary. For if you do not behold God's fierce and overflowing love there at that bitter, bloody tree, you will never see it. For this is none other than the great God himself, a broken, lifeless corpse on that Roman cross.

Surely a love that deep and fierce and fervent and passionate and self-giving has to be at the heart of everything that happens in our lives— the sad and the glad, the bitter and the beautiful. A love like that has to sustain us in every dark and disastrous day, turn every burden into a blessing, and see us gloriously and victoriously through every trial and storm to the joys of heaven.

On the way to Skull Hill they compelled a man to bear the cross for Jesus. Simon didn't volunteer. The soldiers forced that cross on his back.

So it often is with us. God does not give us the luxury of choosing our crosses. In his infinite and unsearchable wisdom and love he selects just the right cross for us, the one he knows we can carry, the one he is sure will enrich our lives.

But sometimes, in a rare burst of commitment, of heroic and sacrificial love, we do choose to carry some crosses. Compassionately we rush to the side of a brother or sister staggering down the road of life beneath a crushing unbearable cross, and we help that burdened person to carry the load. It is then, in those moments when we volunteer to be cross-bearers, that we are the most Christlike. And it is those crosses we choose to carry that can enrich and ennoble us in the most surprising and unexpected ways.

If you're looking for a cross to carry, there are plenty around. Next door sits a lonely widow. Lift that cross of loneliness from her back by a friendly visit or an invitation to dinner. Or how about the forgotten folks in nursing homes? Are there no crosses on their backs that you can help carry just by your presence at their side or by lending them your listening ear? Or how about the people near and far who bear the cross of poverty and oppression? When will our city streets stop being a *Via Dolorosa* down which hurting, hungry, and burdened people stagger, carrying their crosses of unspeakable misery, crosses we have laid on their shoulders by our greed, apathy, and oppression?

And so at last the crucifixion detail arrived at the hill of execution. As was customary, they offered the condemned man a sedative before they began to drive the nails home. But he refused to take it. Why? Is it because sedatives and tranquilizers are strictly forbidden and the taking of them contrary to God's will? Does the consumption of medication for your nerves reveal and betray a small or weak faith? Of course not! If the doctor prescribes the medication, take it and rejoice in its help. Only beware that you do not dull or deaden your sensitivities to the hurts and sorrows of those around you. While it is true there is no moral value in the continuous laceration of our feelings, it is also true that by deadening our pains, making use of mental chloroform, and by drugging our spirits, we can keep our lives from being exposed to costly sympathy and love, and thereby also prevent them from being exposed to the Spirit of God.

At Skull Hill there was some gambling. Here the greatest event of history was unfolding before their very eyes, and all those soldiers could do was to shoot dice. Of course, they couldn't be blamed for not discerning the death of God there on that skull-shaped hill. But they could be faulted, perhaps, for being so cold, calloused, and indifferent in the face of such pain and sorrow.

Yet who are we to condemn? Thousands about us continue to die the slow, agonizing death of starvation. People are in pain everywhere, and all the while the feverish playing of the stock market goes on, the clamorous clutch for more profits, more goods, more power and advantage. It is the latest chapter in the sad and continuous story that began at Calvary—gambling at the foot of the cross.

At Skull Hill there was a glaring misconception of greatness. "Save yourself," they shouted, "and we'll believe in you." Poor misguided mockers! They couldn't conceive of greatness in any other terms than self-gain, self-advantage, self-preservation. Somehow it never dawned on them that the best-preserved thing on this planet is an Egyptian mummy. Yet what could be more dead?

True life, real life, true victory, real power are to be found and possessed only in life-losing, self-giving love. In God's book you have to lose to win, and die to live—as did his only Son for us all.

Finally, we note that "Aha!" is not the last word. That was the word of insult and mockery uttered by those who passed by that crucified man on that Friday long ago. As the sun set on the ghastly scene, that word of derision did indeed seem most fitting and appropriate. But the returns are never in by sunset. A day passed, and then another. And the third day dawned. The grave was empty. The crucified Man lived again, and death was swallowed up in his resurrection victory.

And so, rest assured, my burdened, embattled people. "Aha!" is never the final word—not with the God of Easter around.

7
GOOD FRIDAY

When God
Was Executed

³³And when the sixth hour had come, there was darkness over the whole land until the ninth hour. ³⁴And at the ninth hour Jesus cried with a loud voice, "Eloi, Eloi, lama sabachthani?" which means, "My God, my God, why hast thou forsaken me?" ³⁵And some of the bystanders hearing it said, "Behold, he is calling Elijah." ³⁶And one ran and, filling a sponge full of vinegar, put it on a reed and gave it to him to drink, saying, "Wait, let us see whether Elijah will come to take him down." ³⁷And Jesus uttered a loud cry, and breathed his last. ³⁸And the curtain of the temple was torn in two, from top to bottom. ³⁹And when the centurion, who stood facing him, saw that he thus breathed his last, he said, "Truly this man was the Son of God!"

⁴⁰There were also women looking on from afar, among whom were Mary Magdalene, and Mary the mother of James the younger and of Joses, and Salome, ⁴¹who, when he was in Galilee, followed him, and ministered to him; and also many other women who came up with him to Jerusalem.

⁴²And when evening had come, since it was the day of Preparation, that is, the day before the sabbath, ⁴³Joseph of Arimathea, a respected member of the council, who was also himself looking for the kingdom of God, took courage and went to Pilate, and asked for the body of Jesus. ⁴⁴And Pilate wondered if he were already dead; and summoning the centurion, he asked him whether he was already dead. ⁴⁵And when he learned from the centurion that he was dead, he granted the body to Joseph. ⁴⁶And he bought a linen shroud, and taking him down, wrapped him in the linen shroud, and laid him in a tomb which had been hewn out of the rock; and he rolled a stone against the door of the tomb. ⁴⁷Mary Magdalene and Mary the mother of Joses saw where he was laid.

Mark 15:33-47

Here is how it was *when God was executed*. (*Read Mark 15:33-47*.)

There was great darkness. One sun was mourning for another. The sun in the sky was grieving for the Son on the tree, that blazing heavenly ball hiding his blushing and embarrassed face from the ghastly scene on Golgotha.

Or is this a mini-judgment day? The prophet predicts that the sun will be darkened and the moon become blood red before that great and terrible day, that final and fiery day of the Lord. Every eclipse of sun or moon is an unmistakable cosmic warning for us: "Get ready for your death or the world's end. Either can come in the blinking of an eye."

For that man on the middle cross the darkness was sheer hell. It was the outer darkness of which he so often spoke, the darkness where there is no light at all, not even that of God— only the unbearable loneliness of hell, the terrors, torments, horrors, and agonies of the doomed and the damned, the sufferings, sorrows, and tortures of those abandoned, forsaken, and deserted by God.

When God was executed, there was a cry from that man on the middle tree: "My God, my God, why have you forsaken me?" This is the last recorded word of Jesus in the gospel of Mark. And it is a word of utter misery, the cry of a man who has lost everything—his clothes, his dignity, his friends, his life, his God—tormented, terrified, dying alone in the darkness.

This is also a cry of mystery. Why, Lord,
why? He simply couldn't comprehend or understand. Do you know the feeling? There you
are in the midst of all those insufferable agonies
and sorrows of life—battered, bruised, and
bloodied—and like that dying man on Calvary,
you hurl your anguished *whys* heavenward. And
there is no answer, only stony silence. And so
you go to the cross and look up into the tor-
tured, terrified face of that crucified Christ and
once again remember that this is the great God
himself dying for you, so deep and fierce and
passionate and fervent is his love for you. And
you are strengthened in the unshakable convic-
tion that a love like that could never abandon
or forsake you, could never lay on your back
burdens heavier than you can bear, and will
eventually turn your dark, bitter, and gloomy
Good Friday into a bright, joyful, and triumphant Easter morning.

This cry of our Lord from the cross is also a
shout of mercy. He is left alone, abandoned,
forsaken in the darkness so that you never will
be. The cry of that crucified, deserted Savior
guarantees God's great, strong arms around you
forever. Is not this the promise we hear from
the lips of the Lord: "I will never leave you nor
forsake you"? There are five *nevers* in that

promise. Here is how the words should be translated: "I will *never*, *never* leave you. I will *never*, no *never*, no *never* forsake you." Now God just can't make it any stronger, any more comforting, convincing, reassuring than that. And to think that it's all true only because that man on the middle cross was left alone in the darkness.

When God was executed, the temple curtain was torn in two. Oh, the mercy of God! Only the curtain was destroyed and not the whole temple, the entire city and land. In understandable and completely justified wrath God could have wiped them out and blown them away— Jews, Gentiles, Israel, Rome, the entire planet—for the unforgivably heinous crime of killing his Son. Instead all he did was to tear the temple curtain. What grace, what love, what forgiveness!

And so it still is. All he does is to destroy temple curtains, when justice demands that he blast to bits the entire planet. What grace, what love, what forgiveness! But, of course, that is precisely why this man hangs, suffers, bleeds, and dies on the Calvary tree, so that only temple curtains might be destroyed and not entire temples or races or worlds.

But there is more to be said. That temple curtain separated the holy God from unholy people. Jesus Christ dies on that cross, down comes the dividing curtain, and God and people are together again. The barrier of sin is removed and gone. God embraces us in his arms and hugs us to his heart. We are home again.

There's still more. If Christ's death means that the separating curtain is down, how then can we act and live as if it is still there—separating ourselves from those about us by all our ugly prejudices and bigotries, building walls and fences around ourselves, thereby telling those we consider inferior to keep their distance? Whenever the "us-and-them" mentality takes over, we are forgetting that the curtain came down when he died on Calvary.

When God was executed, a centurion had his eyes opened. He recognized God in this dying man.

Is that how people come to know that we are God's sons and daughters? Can they discern that by the way we both live and die? Can they determine our divine childship by the way we live, by the Christlike love that shines from all that we are and say and do? And can they also discern our divine childship by the way we die, die daily to ourselves, to our godless drives and desires so that we might live in self-giving love for others? Can they see we are God's sons and daughters by the way we die, by the courage and calm, the peace and faith, the resignation and even joy with which we face death? If our eyes are on that crucified and risen Savior, then the eyes of those about us will be opened. And they will see that we are God's faith-filled and love-filled sons and daughters.

When God was executed, some friends buried him. The interment was in a stranger's tomb, not the family grave plot. What a disgrace and dishonor! No room for that disgraceful and dishonorable wretch, that executed criminal in the hallowed family cemetery.

And yet how true to form it all was. As in life, so in death he did not have a home, a place to call his own. Birds had nests, foxes had dens, but the homeless Jesus had no place to lay his weary head. Orphaned to the end, homeless, fatherless, forsaken, buried in a stranger's grave—that we might pray "Abba, Father," and call heaven our home.

And so they buried him and then rolled a great stone before the door. And there the stone stayed—forever. Nonsense! For only three days. On Easter morning away it rolled from the door of that deserted, empty, and conquered tomb to become the park bench from which the angel herald announced the great, glad, good news of his resurrection victory.

8
EASTER

Good News
from the Graveyard

¹And when the sabbath was past, Mary Magdalene, and Mary the mother of James, and Salome, bought spices, so that they might go and anoint him. ²And very early on the first day of the week they went to the tomb when the sun had risen. ³And they were saying to one another, "Who will roll away the stone for us from the door of the tomb?" ⁴And looking up, they saw that the stone was rolled back—it was very large. ⁵And entering the tomb, they saw a young man sitting on the right side, dressed in a white robe; and they were amazed. ⁶And he said to them, "Do not be amazed; you seek Jesus of Nazareth, who was crucified. He has risen, he is not here; see the place where they laid him.

⁷But go, tell his disciples and Peter that he is going before you to Galilee; there you will see him, as he told you." ⁸And they went out and fled from the tomb; for trembling and astonishment had come upon them; and they said nothing to any one, for they were afraid.

Mark 16:1-8

As strange as it sounds, there's *good news from the graveyard*. (*Read Mark 16:1-8*.)

First of all, remember that the Sabbath will pass. Sabbath means *rest*. That's what the women in the Easter story did. They observed the Sabbath, did the prescribed resting on the day after their Master's death. And when the rest day was over, they trudged out to the cemetery, expecting to find him still resting in his grave. But he wasn't. His Sabbath, his rest, in the tomb was over, and out he came from that gloomy garden grotto raised, alive, and triumphant.

As it was for him, so it will be for us. The Sabbath will pass; our rest in the tomb will come to an end; and, like him, we will wake and rise to join our loved ones, friends, and all the saints at God's eternal party.

The second piece of good news from the graveyard is that some marvelous surprises await God's faithful people.

That's how it was with those women on the way to the tomb. How faithful they were, faithful to the bitter end of Good Friday and beyond! And behold how God rewarded their faithfulness with the surprise of their lives, the surprise of that empty tomb.

One wonders what Easter surprises, what unexpected joys, gifts, and blessings our God might have in store for us if we, like those women in the Easter story, will just stay faithfully at it, will not toss in the towel or throw in the sponge, will not surrender to dark despair regardless of the burdens that must be borne, the battles that must be fought, the challenges that must be met, the obstacles that must be overcome, and the failures and defeats that must be suffered.

Here is another piece of good news from the graveyard: no stone is too big to be rolled away. The women were worried about that big boulder that guarded the grave of their dead Master. They knew they couldn't roll it away. Their fears were unfounded. When they arrived at the grave, they saw that the stone was gone. The

Easter angel had sent it rolling from the door of that deserted, conquered, and empty tomb.

Are there any stones in your-life? Sometimes the stones are before and around us. The stones are the obstacles and barriers that we cannot budge or move. The stones of sorrow surround us, encircle us, enclose and imprison us, and there is no hope of escape or deliverance. Who will roll the stones away?

And sometimes we are under the stones. The sorrows and crosses and burdens are so great and large and heavy that, like stones, they crush all life and hope and joy and faith and strength and courage right out of us. Who will roll the stones away?

And at last we will lie dead under a stone, the gravestone with our name on it. Surely that is an immovable stone. Surely no one can roll that stone away and restore life to the buried body beneath it.

Go to the garden, and with the women behold that stone sent rolling from the door of that open, empty, and conquered grave. And now you know that no stone in your life, however huge and heavy, will be there forever. The Easter angel is still around, and his arm has lost none of its strength or power.

on uses biblical texts about suffering
ffering of Jesus to respond to ques-
tians face today. A fine book for use
Lenten season, it also is a biblical
mfort for all those who suffer.

he Theology of the Cross by Peter L.

bing book interprets Luther's the-
e cross and proclaims the God who
lom in foolishness and strength in
Steinke uses nine passages from the
ow how the cross of Christ puts all
le test.

l of Lent by Robert Kysar

ifixion of Jesus presented a tremen-
bling block for Jews and Gentiles of
tury, a scandal Christians have often
nimize. Kysar's in-depth interpre-
es the paradoxes of selected passages
el of John, emphasizing the points
sus challenges our refined sensibil-
ks us to believe.

And so two words begin to disappear from our minds and mouths: *hopeless* and *impossible*. For if God can do even that—roll stones from grave doors, open tombs, and bring back the dead—then anything is possible, anything great and grand and glorious. Now no sorrow, death, or grave can last forever—not with the God of Easter around to do his stone-rolling resurrection thing. And the dying embers of hope begin to burn, blaze, and glow brightly again.

Good news from the graveyard. "He has risen," said the heavenly herald to those women standing dumbfounded in the darkness of that empty tomb. Out he came from that gloomy garden grave to be our coffin-conqueror and death-destroyer.

He has risen, and so have you. By way of that Word-and-water miracle called Baptism you rose with your Lord at the crack of that first Easter dawn and have already been delivered from the only death we ever need to fear: the death of endless separation from our God.

He has risen, and so are you, rising each day from the death of sin and evil to a new life of righteousness and love. By the power that flows into you from that crucified and risen Man in gospel Word and communion bread and wine, you rise above it all, rise above your doubts and fears, your burdens and defeats to live the life of Easter, a life of hope and courage and peace and faithfulness and joy.

He has risen, and so will you. Of course, it's no fun to enter the cocoon. Just ask that creeping caterpillar. It's dark in that cocoon. It's lonely there. What assurance does he have that he won't stay there forever? What assurance that he will ever rise again? But like it or not, into the cocoon he goes, there to abide and remain for a while. And then it happens, resurrection morning, and out he comes a brand new, beautiful butterfly.

Easter joyfully proclaims that one butterfly has already emerged from the cocoon of the grave. And so, my fellow caterpillars, as we creep and crawl inevitably toward the cocoon, we do so always with hope in our hearts, fixing our gaze on that resurrected butterfly, who, having conquered the coffin and the grave, legitimately calls himself the Resurrection and the Life and invites us to cling confidently to him as we enter our coffin-cocoons, there to sleep only for a little while until at the summons of our Savior we fly forth from our rent cocoons on resurrection morning as God's brand new beautiful butterflies. And then it's good-bye and farewell to cocoons forever.

And so two words begin to disappear from our minds and mouths: *hopeless* and *impossible*. For if God can do even that—roll stones from grave doors, open tombs, and bring back the dead—then anything is possible, anything great and grand and glorious. Now no sorrow, death, or grave can last forever—not with the God of Easter around to do his stone-rolling resurrection thing. And the dying embers of hope begin to burn, blaze, and glow brightly again.

Good news from the graveyard. "He has risen," said the heavenly herald to those women standing dumbfounded in the darkness of that empty tomb. Out he came from that gloomy garden grave to be our coffin-conqueror and death-destroyer.

He has risen, and so have you. By way of that Word-and-water miracle called Baptism you rose with your Lord at the crack of that first Easter dawn and have already been delivered from the only death we ever need to fear: the death of endless separation from our God.

He has risen, and so are you, rising each day from the death of sin and evil to a new life of righteousness and love. By the power that flows into you from that crucified and risen Man in gospel Word and communion bread and wine, you rise above it all, rise above your doubts and fears, your burdens and defeats to live the life of Easter, a life of hope and courage and peace and faithfulness and joy.

He has risen, and so will you. Of course, it's no fun to enter the cocoon. Just ask that creeping caterpillar. It's dark in that cocoon. It's lonely there. What assurance does he have that he won't stay there forever? What assurance that he will ever rise again? But like it or not, into the cocoon he goes, there to abide and remain for a while. And then it happens, resurrection morning, and out he comes a brand new, beautiful butterfly.

Easter joyfully proclaims that one butterfly has already emerged from the cocoon of the grave. And so, my fellow caterpillars, as we creep and crawl inevitably toward the cocoon, we do so always with hope in our hearts, fixing our gaze on that resurrected butterfly, who, having conquered the coffin and the grave, legitimately calls himself the Resurrection and the Life and invites us to cling confidently to him as we enter our coffin-cocoons, there to sleep only for a little while until at the summons of our Savior we fly forth from our rent cocoons on resurrection morning as God's brand new beautiful butterflies. And then it's good-bye and farewell to cocoons forever.

Lenten Resources

The following Lenten resources are available from Augsburg Publishing House:

Meeting Christ in Handel's Messiah by Roger T. Quillin

Seven Lent and Easter messages based on Handel's texts and music from *Messiah* are contained in this unique sermon book. Roger Quillin combines insightful messages on key Bible texts with portions of Handel's magnificent work. A fine series for any size congregation, the musical selections may be performed by a choir or played from a recording.

Where Is God in My Suffering? by Daniel J. Simundson

Simundson uses biblical texts about suffering and the suffering of Jesus to respond to questions Christians face today. A fine book for use during the Lenten season, it also is a biblical book of comfort for all those who suffer.

Preaching the Theology of the Cross by Peter L. Steinke

This probing book interprets Luther's theology of the cross and proclaims the God who shows wisdom in foolishness and strength in weakness. Steinke uses nine passages from the Bible to show how the cross of Christ puts all things to the test.

The Scandal of Lent by Robert Kysar

The crucifixion of Jesus presented a tremendous stumbling block for Jews and Gentiles of the first century, a scandal Christians have often tried to minimize. Kysar's in-depth interpretation studies the paradoxes of selected passages in the gospel of John, emphasizing the points at which Jesus challenges our refined sensibilities, yet asks us to believe.